THE
Christ
OF CHRISTMAS

AN AGE-OLD STORY WITH A *New* FAMILY TRADITION

MARC SIKMA
illustrations by Rita Tan

Brentwood, Tennessee

Dedication

To Heidi, Avery, Dawson, & Maddox:
you are a gracious gift from
the One we love.

ABOUT THE AUTHOR

MARC SIKMA is husband to Heidi and father to Avery, Dawson, and
Maddox. Marc planted Matthias' Lot Church in St. Charles, Missouri
in 2005 and founded the nonprofit, We Love St. Charles in 2009.
Through his church, nonprofit, and now *The Christ of Christmas*,
Marc hopes to empower families with the truth of Jesus, who is
not just the reason for the season—He is the reason for all of life.

Text Copyright © 2023 by Marc Sikma
Illustrations by Rita Tan. Illustrations are inspired by Jordan Moler's work
in the original version of *The Christ of Christmas*.
Illustrations Copyright © 2023 by B&H Publishing Group
Published by B&H Publishing Group, Brentwood, Tennessee
All rights reserved. ISBN: 978-1-0877-7821-1
Scripture references are taken from The Holy Bible, English Standard Version®
Copyright © 2001 by Crossway Bibles, a publishing ministry of Good News Publishers.
Dewey Decimal Classification: C232.3
Subject Heading: CHRISTMAS \ JESUS CHRIST \ CONVERSION
Printed in Shenzhen, Guangdong, China, March 2023
1 2 3 4 5 6 · 27 26 25 24 23

My story begins where
a lot of good stories begin—

Christmas.

I know most people say they love Christmas, but I really, really, *really* love Christmas. Not because of the presents or good food (even though those things are awesome).

My mom is why I love Christmas. I have a *great* dad and a *mostly* cool brother, but my mom is the one who told me something that changed my life forever. And the first time she told me was on Christmas Day.

You see, I was born on December 20th. I guess you could say I was my parents' favorite Christmas gift. On Christmas morning, I was just five days old, and my mom started a new family tradition. She told me about the Christ of Christmas—she told me about Jesus—as she rocked me in her arms, my dad sitting nearby.

"All of us, even you, baby Lilly, have a *big* problem. We start our lives full of sin. Every person worships things other than God, and that means our relationship with God is broken."

Even though I didn't understand, Mom held up a little wooden manger and told me about why Jesus was born.

"God had a plan to heal what was broken. God's Son left heaven and came to earth to make things right! He came as a baby like you, but He was born in a miraculous way. He was placed in a manger that looked kind of like this one. His parents named Him Jesus."

Mom put the manger down and said, "He didn't stay a baby though. Jesus grew up and walked around the world loving people. He taught them, healed them, and cared for them. He showed them who God is, because Jesus *is* God."

Then Mom picked up the second wooden object—a cross. With tears in her eyes, she said, "Lilly, I want to tell you why Jesus had to die.

"God loves us and gives us life, but remember how we have sin in our hearts? When people sin, we reject God's love. The consequence of our sin is death, and God can't overlook our sin—there has to be a consequence. Even though Jesus was God, and He never sinned, He willingly died on a cross that kind of looked like this one.

"He took the consequence for us! God forgives the sin of anyone who believes in Jesus. Best of all, Jesus didn't stay dead. Three days after He died, He defeated death. He came back to life! He is the only person who could be punished for sin by death and then come back to life. And He is *still* alive, Lilly!"

I was just a baby when Mom started
this Christmas-morning tradition.

Year after year, she pulled out the little manger and wooden cross. She always ended the story by saying, "I want you to remember that no matter what . . . in health or hurt . . . nothing changes that Jesus is the Christ of Christmas."

Want to know what's really awesome? This tradition hasn't just been powerful for me. I've seen it impact my brother too.

I was seven when Mom and Dad became foster parents and Zeke joined our family. I was so excited for Zeke to arrive at our house for the first time, but when he walked in, he walked right past me.

According to Dad, I got really upset and shut myself in my room. I'm sure I got over it quickly because it didn't take long for Zeke and me to become friends. Within a few weeks, I felt like he was my brother.

17

As December neared, I said, "Zeke, Christmas around here is really special. Mom is going to tell us about the Christ of Christmas—why Jesus had to be born and why He had to die." Zeke looked confused, but I could tell he wanted to hear more.

The day finally came! Dad sat nearby, and Zeke and I snuggled with Mom as she showed us the little manger and wooden cross and told us about Jesus.

By the next Christmas, our family had adopted Zeke as my official brother. We woke up early, and I ran down the stairs as fast as my feet would take me.

Mom added some things to the story that year. She told us that because of Jesus, God can adopt us into His family. We can have a forever home with Him, and He will never, ever, ever abandon us.

Zeke couldn't stop smiling. "Being adopted by God sounds even better than being adopted by you guys!"

Year after year, Zeke and I grew
older, but Christmas morning
stayed the same—Dad sitting
nearby, Mom with her manger and
wooden cross, and Zeke and me
cuddled up with her on the couch.

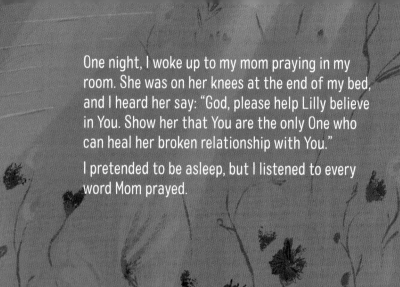

One night, I woke up to my mom praying in my room. She was on her knees at the end of my bed, and I heard her say: "God, please help Lilly believe in You. Show her that You are the only One who can heal her broken relationship with You."

I pretended to be asleep, but I listened to every word Mom prayed.

God must have heard my mom's prayers because not long after that, God's love felt real. I was reading the Bible alone in my room when I saw these words in the book of Romans: "If you confess with your mouth that Jesus is Lord and believe in your heart that God raised him from the dead, you will be saved."

I ran down the hall, grabbed my mom's hand, and pulled her to my room. "Mom! You know how you pray for me to believe in God?"

"Yes, Lilly," she said, smiling from ear to ear. I think she knew what I was about to say.

"Well, I do. I believe! I know He is my God too and not just yours. I want to follow Jesus."

She was soooooo excited, and Zeke was too! He must have heard the celebration because he came running in to join us. Mom said, "Christmas is going to be so different now!"

None of us knew how true Mom's words were. Just two weeks ago, on my birthday, I woke up to my dad standing by my bed.

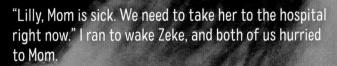

"Lilly, Mom is sick. We need to take her to the hospital right now." I ran to wake Zeke, and both of us hurried to Mom.

"I'm going to be okay. Everything will be fine." Mom's voice sounded raspy and weak as she whispered, "No matter what . . . in health or hurt . . . nothing changes that Jesus is the Christ of Christmas."

At the hospital, the doctors ran test after test for days but couldn't figure out what was wrong. *Why can't they just fix her?* I thought. *Why can't God just fix her?* I was worried, Zeke was scared, and I saw tears roll down my dad's cheeks for the first time.

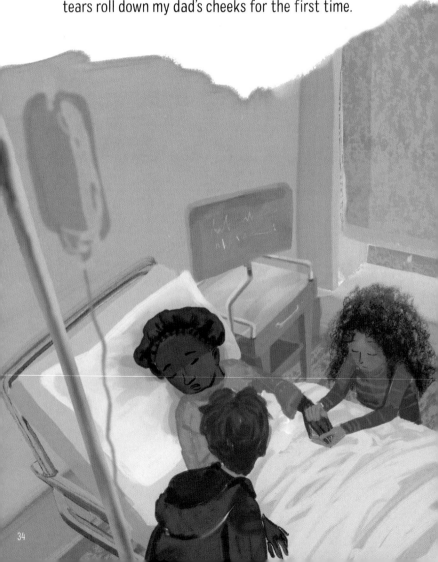

By Christmas Eve, we had barely slept, and Mom hadn't woken up. Dad decided it was time to go home and rest. I grabbed Mom's hand and prayed for God to heal her broken body, just like all those nights she prayed for God to heal my heart. Mom was right. Christmas was different this year.

When we got home, I went to the mantel where Mom kept the manger and wooden cross. I clutched them next to my heart and remembered all the years Mom held them.

I took a deep breath and decided that this Christmas, I would be the one to share about Jesus. I gave my dad a hug, told Zeke good night, and prayed for God to work a miracle in my family.

When I woke up on Christmas morning, my heart felt heavy. I didn't yell for Zeke, and I didn't run down the stairs. I just wanted to get back to the hospital and bring our Christmas tradition to Mom. But when I went to the mantel, the manger and wooden cross were gone.

No, no, no.

I scoured the room, but I couldn't find them anywhere.

This is the year that Mom needs me most, and I lost her favorite part of Christmas.

That's when I found an unexpected scene: Dad was sitting at the table, and he didn't look distraught like he had every day since Mom got sick. He had the happiest, most exhausted-looking grin on his face.

"Go get Zeke," he said. "It's time to celebrate Christmas with Mom."

The car ride to the hospital was different. Instead of sitting in silence like the night before, Dad made us sing out-of-tune Christmas carols and plan how we were going to make Mom's day special.

Mom was still sick, I couldn't believe I lost the manger and cross, and we were sad, but something was different. Dad seemed different.

When the car slowed to a stop, the three of us rushed into the hospital where we met Mom's doctor in the hallway. He looked stunned.

I started to panic.

Did something happen in the night? Had Mom gotten worse? I even started to think, *Did Mom . . .*

"Your mom is awake." The doctor cut my
thoughts off. "She woke up this morning, and
I don't know how, but she is going to be okay."

I'm not proud that Zeke and I got scolded by
more than one nurse as we darted down the
hall and burst into Mom's room. Like a normal
Christmas, there she sat—ready for us.

I will never, ever forget the first words out of her mouth that morning: "No matter what . . . in health or hurt . . . nothing changes that Jesus is the Christ of Christmas."

It felt like we hugged forever. Zeke, Dad, Mom, and I held each other, laughing and crying. That's when Dad asked us all to sit down. He reached into his pocket and pulled them out—the manger and cross! Mom's eyes widened, and mine filled with tears. Dad's smile that morning, the look on his face when I saw him with the wooden objects in his hands—I knew where this was going.

"Last night, I couldn't stop crying." Dad squeezed Mom's hand. "I was sad about you, sad about my life, and terrified our kids would lose their mom and I would lose my wife. But through my tears, I saw this little manger and wooden cross. It's hard to put into words, but something happened to me in that moment.

"I've watched you have faith in God, and I thought that since I was a good person, I didn't really need faith. But I was still so empty."

Then he turned to Zeke and me and said, "Kids, late last night, God spoke to me through your mom. All these years, as she's held up this little manger and wooden cross, I was glad she was telling you about Jesus. But she was telling me too."

With a lump in his throat and joy in his voice, Dad looked at my mom (who was a puddle of tears) and said, "I spent the whole morning praying I would get the chance to tell you these words: I believe. I believe my relationship with God is broken. I believe I need Jesus to save me, and I believe that He died and rose again! I believe that trusting in Him is the only way to heal my relationship with God. My love, from this day forward, I will follow Jesus."

For the first time in my life, *Dad* used those two wooden pieces to tell us about the hope Jesus brings.

He told us why Jesus had to be born, why Jesus had to die, and how He could heal our broken relationship with God. Dad repeated the words he'd listened to my mom share for years.

The four of us celebrated! Right there, on Christmas morning, around my mom's hospital bed, God healed my mom's broken body and my dad's broken heart.

My name is Lilly. I'm a child of God, and so are my mom *and* dad. My mom's body was healed that day, but even if it wasn't, Jesus would still be the Christ of Christmas. I believe God has special plans for each of our lives.

I can't wait to spend the rest of my life telling everyone this truth: through a humble manger and a wooden cross, God heals our broken relationships with Him.

My family is forever changed. Not because of a holiday or an amazing tradition, but because no matter what . . . in health or hurt . . . nothing changes that Jesus is the Christ of *Christmas.*

Remember

Therefore, if anyone is in Christ, he is a new creation. The old has passed away; behold, the new has come.—2 Corinthians 5:17

Read

In Luke 19:1-10, Jesus encountered a man named Zacchaeus who needed to be made new. He was a sinner, but his interaction with Jesus changed Zacchaeus' life forever. Jesus saved him from his sins, and Zacchaeus was never the same again.

Like Zacchaeus, we all need a Savior. Our sin separates us from God and keeps us from enjoying a relationship with Him. But God, being rich in mercy, sent Jesus to forgive our sins, heal our hearts, and make us new. All we have to do is believe in Jesus. Lilly's family is an example for us. Her mom patiently and consistently shared the gospel with her family, and her dad was transformed by Jesus from the inside out. What a remarkable change! His "old" self had gone away and the new had come!

Think

1. What was your favorite moment in the story of Lilly's family? How did you feel when you read about that moment?

2. Family traditions are one way we can celebrate what Jesus has done! How does your family celebrate? What is one Jesus-centered tradition you'd like to do with your family in the future?

3. Read pages 8-13 of *The Christ of Christmas* again. How does this story encourage you and bring you joy?

4. Who is someone you can share Christ with? Say a prayer they would want to be made new!